SPOTLIGHT ON SPACE SCIENCE

JOURNEY THROUGH ECLIPSES

CAROLYN L. HILL

New York

Published in 2015 by The Rosen Publishing Group, Inc.
29 East 21st Street, New York, NY 10010

First Edition

Editor: Susan Meyer
Book Design: Kris Everson

Photo Credits: Cover (main) NASA/Goddard Space Flight Center Scientific Visualization Studio; cover (eclipses) Brian Paczkowski; pp. 4, 15, 23 Shutterstock.com; p. 5 Alan Dyer/Stocktrek Images/ Getty Images; p. 7 (Earth) NASA; p. 7 (moon) NASA/JPL/USGS; pp. 7 (Sun), 9 NASA/SDO/AIA/HMI/ Goddard Space Flight Center; p. 11 NASA/Bill Dunford; p. 13 Ruby Tuesday Books, Ltd.; pp. 16, 20, 26 Ruby Tuesday Books, Ltd./Shutterstock.com; p. 17 NASA's Goddard Space Flight Center Scientific Visualization Studio; p. 19 Mark Stevenson/Stocktrek Images/Getty Images; pp. 21, 25 NASA/ Getty Images; p. 27 Tobias Roetsch/Stocktrek Images/Getty Images; p. 29 NASA/JPL-Caltech/SSI.

Library of Congress Cataloging-in-Publication Data

Hill, Carolyn L.
Journey through eclipses / by Carolyn L. Hill.
p. cm. — (Spotlight on space science)
Includes index.
ISBN 978-1-4994-0377-0 (pbk.)
ISBN 978-1-4994-0406-7 (6-pack)
ISBN 978-1-4994-0430-2 (library binding)
1. Solar eclipses — Juvenile literature. 2. Lunar eclipses — Juvenile literature. I. Hill, Carolyn L. II. Title.
QB541.5 H55 2015
523.7—d23

Manufactured in the United States of America

CPSIA Compliance Information: Batch #CW15PK: For Further Information contact Rosen Publishing, New York, New York at 1-800-237-9932

CONTENTS

A STRANGE PHENOMENON

CHAPTER 1

It is early morning in the city of Varanasi, India. The Sun rises into the sky over the Ganges River. Thousands of people are waiting on the banks of the river. The

People wait on the banks of the Ganges for the eclipse to begin.

dawn sky is light, but suddenly the skies become dark. The Moon has covered the Sun, blocking its light and turning day to night!

On July 22, 2009, the people on the banks of the Ganges in Varanasi experienced an amazing event—a total eclipse of the Sun. This amazing **phenomenon** was not just witnessed at Varanasi, but in many parts of Asia, too. In some places, day turned to night for several minutes.

From Earth, it's possible to witness eclipses of the Sun, called **solar** eclipses, and eclipses of the Moon, called **lunar** eclipses. So, what exactly happens during an eclipse, and what causes these amazing **astronomical** events to take place?

EARTH, THE SUN, AND THE MOON

CHAPTER 2

Before we get started on the science that makes solar and lunar eclipses happen, let's take a closer look at the three bodies involved—our Earth, the Moon, and the Sun.

Earth is a **planet**. It's a round, rocky ball that **orbits**, or moves around, the Sun.

The Sun is the nearest **star** to Earth. This giant ball of burning gases provides all the light and heat that makes life on Earth possible. The Sun is many times larger than Earth. In fact, about 1.3 million Earths could fit inside the Sun! The Sun is also a very long way from Earth—about 93 million miles (150 million km).

The Moon is a rocky ball that orbits Earth from an average distance of about 238,855 miles (384,400 km) away. It is much smaller than Earth. About 81 Moons could fit inside Earth.

Earth is larger than the Moon. In fact, four Moons could fit across our planet. However, the Sun is by far the largest body in the solar system. It is so wide that 109 Earths could fit across it. Earth and the Moon are shown to scale, but the Sun is not. Compared to Earth, the Sun would be far larger than shown here.

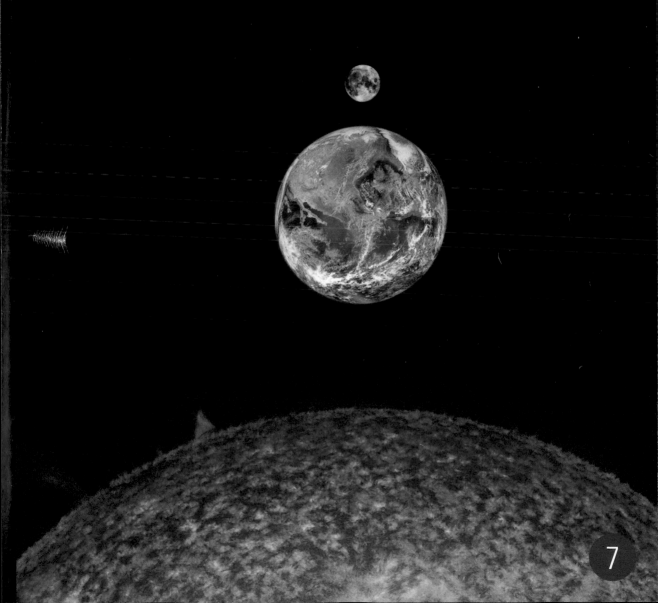

ALWAYS ORBITING

CHAPTER 3

When we study eclipses, it's important to understand how Earth, the Moon, and the Sun interact with each other.

The Moon is orbiting Earth. It makes one complete orbit of Earth every 27.3 days. As the Moon orbits Earth, it follows an elliptical, or oval, pathway. As the Moon moves in its orbit, it at times is close to Earth and at times is far from Earth. These two points are called the **perigee** (when the Moon is closest to Earth) and the **apogee** (when it is farthest away).

Earth is orbiting the Sun. It makes one full orbit of the Sun every 365 days—the time period that we call a year.

For billions of years, the Moon has been orbiting Earth, and together, the Moon and Earth have been orbiting the Sun. This relationship between

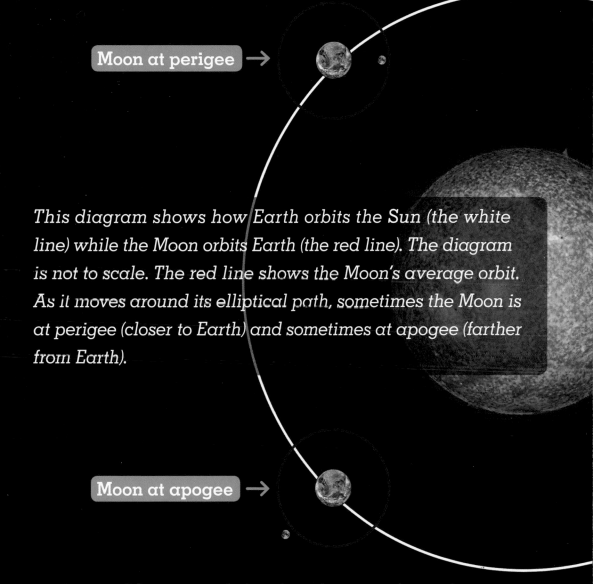

Moon at perigee →

This diagram shows how Earth orbits the Sun (the white line) while the Moon orbits Earth (the red line). The diagram is not to scale. The red line shows the Moon's average orbit. As it moves around its elliptical path, sometimes the Moon is at perigee (closer to Earth) and sometimes at apogee (farther from Earth).

Moon at apogee →

Earth, the Moon, and the Sun is one of the factors that make it possible for eclipses to happen.

9

THE PHASES OF THE MOON
CHAPTER 4

Sometimes the Moon looks like a giant white disk. This is known as a **full moon**. At other times, it becomes a thin crescent. The changing views of the Moon are called phases.

A lunar eclipse can only occur when there is a full moon. Let's look at what causes a full moon to happen.

As the Moon orbits Earth, different parts of the Moon catch the Sun's light. The diagram (right) shows the Moon making one orbit of Earth. The inner ring of small Moons shows how the Sun's light hits the Moon's surface. The outer ring of larger Moons shows what we see from Earth.

When we see a full moon, the Moon is on the side of Earth that is opposite from the Sun. We get to see the whole surface of the Moon that is lit up by the Sun's light.

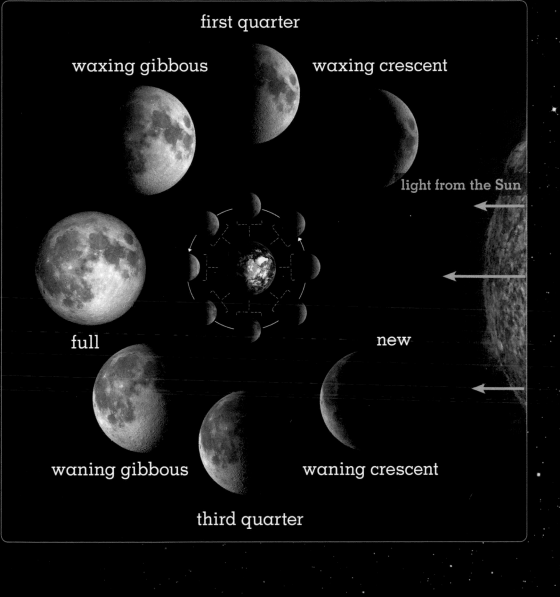

first quarter

waxing gibbous

waxing crescent

light from the Sun

full

new

waning gibbous

waning crescent

third quarter

This diagram shows the Moon's phases (as seen from the northern hemisphere) during one orbit of Earth. The views of the Moon we see from Earth have names, such as "full moon" or "waxing crescent."

THE MOON AND SHADOWS

CHAPTER 5

We've looked at how the Moon orbits Earth and how its appearance changes during different phases. So, what is a lunar eclipse and why does it happen?

As Earth moves around the Sun, it casts two shadows. One is called the **penumbral shadow**, and the other is the **umbral shadow**. Sometimes during its full moon phase, the Moon passes through these shadows (see diagram 1).

The Moon doesn't pass through the shadows on every orbit because its pathway is slightly tilted (see diagram 2). Most of the time, the Moon orbits above or below the shadows cast by Earth. Sometimes, however, the Moon's orbit takes it through Earth's shadows. This is when a lunar eclipse happens.

If a section of the Moon passes through Earth's umbral shadow, we see that section of the Moon become dark. This is called a partial lunar eclipse (see diagram 3).

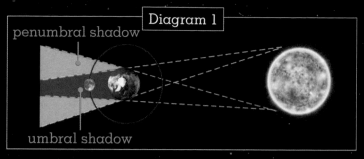

Diagram 1

penumbral shadow

umbral shadow

This diagram shows the Earth's shadows. The diagram is viewed from above and is not to scale.

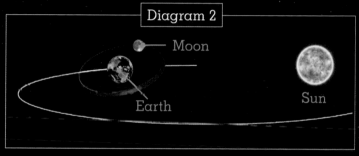

Diagram 2

Moon

Earth

Sun

This diagram shows how the Moon's orbit is slightly tilted to the Earth's orbit.

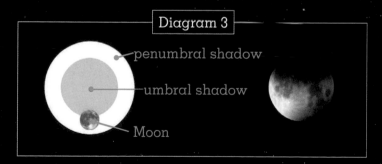

Diagram 3

penumbral shadow

umbral shadow

Moon

If we could see the umbral and penumbral shadows from Earth, they would look like two circles. Here, a section of the Moon passes through the umbral shadow (left). We see this as a partial eclipse (right).

TOTAL LUNAR ECLIPSE

CHAPTER 6

Sometimes the Moon's orbit is just right for the entire Moon to pass through Earth's umbral shadow. Then, a total lunar eclipse occurs.

It might seem that the whole face of the Moon would turn dark during a total eclipse. In fact, something amazing happens. The Moon turns shades of red and orange.

As the Sun's light passes around Earth, Earth's atmosphere bends the light. This enables some of the light to reach the Moon and illuminate it. The Sun's light is made up of many colors. When it passes through a thick layer of Earth's atmosphere, most of the light that makes it through is red. That's why the Moon is lit up in oranges and reds.

This series of images shows the Moon as it passes through the stages of a total lunar eclipse.

If Earth had no atmosphere, the Moon would appear completely black during a total lunar eclipse.

COVERING THE SUN

CHAPTER 7

Solar eclipses can only take place at the time of a new moon when the Moon passes between Earth and the Sun. If the orbits of Earth and the Moon are in just the right position, we see the Moon cover part or all of the Sun.

When the Moon is between the Sun and Earth, it creates a penumbral and an umbral shadow. Most of the time, the Moon's shadows miss Earth. They fall above or below Earth because the Moon's orbit is slightly tilted. Sometimes, however, the Moon's orbit is just right for one of its shadows to fall on Earth.

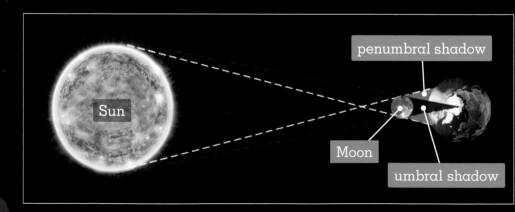

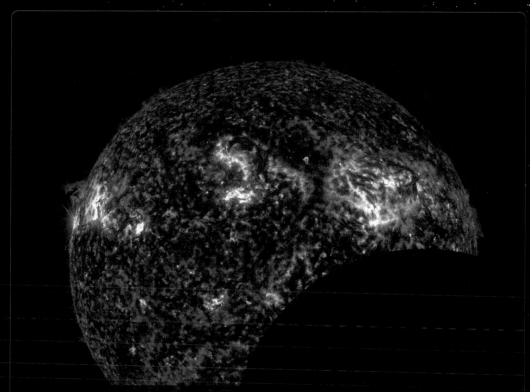

This is a close look at the Sun being eclipsed by the Moon. This photograph was taken by the Solar Dynamics Observatory, a spacecraft orbiting Earth.

When the Moon's penumbral shadow falls on Earth, a partial eclipse happens. From the part of the world where the Moon's shadow falls, it's possible to see the Moon's dark disk covering part of the Sun.

HOW DOES A TOTAL SOLAR ECLIPSE WORK?

CHAPTER 8

Sometimes when the Moon passes between Earth and the Sun, its orbit is positioned just right to cause a total solar eclipse. As the three bodies come perfectly into line, the Moon blocks out all the Sun's light, and day turns to night on Earth!

So how is it possible that from Earth we see the tiny Moon block out the massive Sun?

The math that makes total solar eclipses possible is amazing. The Moon is 400 times smaller than the Sun. The distance between Earth and the Sun, however, is 400 times greater than the distance between Earth and the Moon. This matching up of size and distance makes the Moon exactly the right size to completely eclipse the Sun!

*The black disk in this image is the Moon. During a total
solar eclipse, it falls directly between the Sun and Earth.*

FINDING TOTALITY

CHAPTER 9

During a total solar eclipse, the Moon's umbral shadow falls on just a small section of Earth. This area is called the path of totality. From this area, it's possible to see the Moon completely block out the Sun.

The path of totality is generally about 10,000 miles (16,000 km) long. It is usually only about 100 miles (160 km) wide, though. In order to witness a total eclipse, a person must be inside the path of totality.

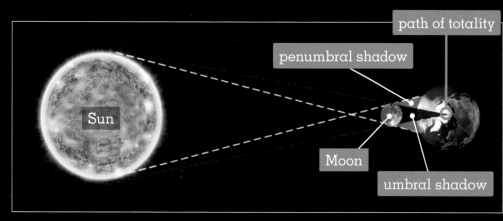

This diagram shows how the Moon's umbral shadow creates the path of totality.

A total eclipse can happen anywhere on Earth. It only happens, however, about once every two years. Astronomers, scientists, space fans, and TV film crews will travel across the world for the chance to see and record this amazing phenomenon!

This dark spot on Earth's surface marks the area where viewers see a total eclipse. People just outside of this shadow witness a partial eclipse.

AN INCREDIBLE EXPERIENCE

CHAPTER 10

Most people who have been lucky enough to witness a total solar eclipse say that it is a truly awesome experience!

As crowds of people stare at the sky through special protective glasses, the dark disk of the Moon slowly moves across the face of the Sun. At the moment of totality, the Moon moves precisely into place to block out the Sun's light.

Daytime turns to night and stars appear. Birds become quiet and stop flying around. Many animals get ready to go to sleep. The temperature may drop by up to 60 degrees Fahrenheit (16 degrees Celsius). Then after a few minutes, the edge of the Sun appears as the Moon continues on its course.

You should never look directly at the Sun because it will permanently damage your eyes. When viewing solar eclipses, you should wear specially designed eye protectors.

WHAT IS THE CORONA?

CHAPTER 11

As the burning disk of the Sun disappears during a total solar eclipse, the Sun's beautiful corona appears. The corona is a layer of gases that surrounds the Sun.

The corona is not normally visible, so total eclipses give scientists an important opportunity to study this part of the Sun. One of the mysteries they want to solve is this: How can the corona be so much hotter than the Sun's surface?

The Sun's corona has a temperature of around 1.8 million degrees Fahrenheit (1 million degrees Celsius). In places, it can reach 20 times this temperature. The surface of the Sun, however, is just 10,000 degrees Fahrenheit (5,500 degrees Celsius). It's like the air around a light bulb being thousands of times hotter than the surface of the bulb!

As the Moon slides in front of the Sun, the Sun's powerful corona is revealed. The corona extends far beyond the star's edge.

Every total solar eclipse that occurs gives scientists a chance to try to solve the mystery of what makes the Sun's corona so hot.

ALMOST TOTALITY

CHAPTER 12

Sometimes when a solar eclipse occurs, the Moon's disk almost blocks out the whole Sun, but not quite. This type of eclipse is known as an annular eclipse.

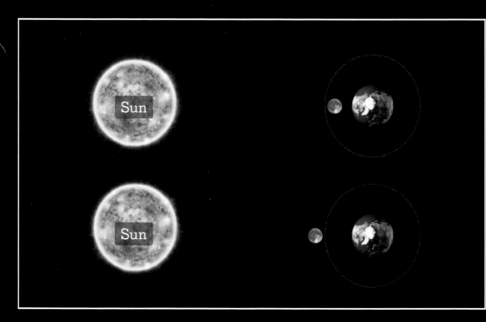

When the Moon is at perigee in its orbit (top diagram), a total solar eclipse can happen. When the Moon is at apogee (bottom diagram), an annular eclipse can happen. This diagram is viewed from above and is not to scale.

When a total eclipse occurs, the Moon has passed between the Sun and Earth near perigee, the closest point to Earth in its orbit. This closeness makes the Moon appear large enough to block out the Sun.

Sometimes, however, an eclipse occurs when the Moon is near apogee, the farthest point from Earth in its orbit. This is when an annular eclipse happens. The Moon is farther away from Earth, so it doesn't appear large enough to completely block out the Sun. The Moon almost covers the Sun, but a bright ring of sunlight can still be seen surrounding the dark disk of the Moon.

This photograph shows an annular solar eclipse in Africa.

THE FUTURE OF ECLIPSES ON EARTH

CHAPTER 13

Earth is not the only planet in our solar system that has a moon and experiences eclipses. In fact, there are over 150 known moons in the solar system. Our Moon is the only one, however, that can cause a total eclipse of the Sun!

This won't always be the case, though. The Moon is slowly drifting away from Earth at about 1.6 inches (4 cm) every year. A billion years from now, the Moon may no longer be at just the right distance to ever completely block out all the Sun's light. This means there will be no more total solar eclipses on Earth.

We are lucky enough to be on this planet at a moment in its history when it's possible to enjoy the amazing event that is a total solar eclipse. So put on those protective glasses, look to the skies, and enjoy!

This is what a solar eclipse looks like from one of the moons of Saturn. The gas giant has crossed in front of the Sun, and its rings and atmosphere are glowing because of the sunlight shining behind them. The image was captured by the Cassini space probe as it orbited Saturn.

GLOSSARY

apogee: The point in the Moon's orbit that is farthest from Earth.

astronomical: Having to do with astronomy, which is the science that deals with space objects beyond Earth.

full moon: The phase of the Moon when the whole disk is lit up by the Sun.

lunar: Having to do with the Moon.

orbit: To move around an object along a curved path; also, the curved path of a space object around a star, planet, or moon.

penumbral shadow: A shadow cast where the light is partly but not wholly cut off by the blocking body.

perigee: The point in the Moon's orbit that is closest to Earth.

phenomenon: Something that can be observed and studied and that typically is unusual or difficult to understand or explain fully.

planet: A space object that orbits around a star.

solar: Having to do with the Sun.

star: A space object made of gases that produces its own light.

umbral shadow: A shadow cast where all light is cut off by the blocking body.

FOR MORE INFORMATION

BOOKS

Hughes, Catherine D. *First Big Book of Space.* Washington, D.C.: National Geographic, 2012.

Hunter, Nick. *Eclipses*. Portsmouth, NH: Heinemann Library, 2013.

Portman, Michael. *What Is an Eclipse?* New York, NY: Gareth Stevens Publishing, 2014.

WEBSITES

Due to the changing nature of Internet links, PowerKids Press has developed an online list of websites related to the subject of this book. This site is updated regularly. Please use this link to access the list: www.powerkidslinks.com/soss/ecli

INDEX